THE SCARLET PIMPERNEL

Baroness Emmuska Orczy

AUTHORED by Soman Chainani
UPDATED AND REVISED by W.C. Miller

COVER DESIGN by Table XI Partners LLC
COVER PHOTO by Olivia Verma and © 2005 GradeSaver, LLC

BOOK DESIGN by Table XI Partners LLC

Published by GradeSaver LLC, www.gradesaver.com

First published in the United States of America by GradeSaver LLC. 2007

GRADESAVER, the GradeSaver logo and the phrase "Getting you the grade since 1999" are registered trademarks of GradeSaver, LLC

ISBN 978-1-60259-093-9

Printed in the United States of America

For other products and additional information please visit
http://www.gradesaver.com

Table of Contents

Table of Contents

Biography of Orczy, Emmuska Baroness (1865-1947)

Baroness Orczy was born Emmuska Magdalena Rosalia Maria Josefa Barbara Orczy, an aristocrat in Hungary to a baron and former countess. Initially she lived a life of luxury and prestige, as her father occupied a place in the court of the Austro-Hungarian empire. Her father, Baron Felix Orczy, was a minor composer. He presided over the family estate 'Tarna Ors,' where great composers like Wagner, Liszt and Gounod used to visit.

However, when the Baroness' father attempted to modernize his tenants' farming methods, a peasant revolt broke out and the family fled -- first to Brussels, then Paris, and ultimately to London. There, the Baroness studied at the West London School of Art, where she fell in love with Montague Barstow. The two married in 1894, and ended up being creative collaborators. They produced a translation of Hungarian folktales which went on to great success, allowing Orczy to continue writing.

Orczy's first novel, *The Emperor's Candlesticks*, was rejected for being too short, so she went back to smaller scale work like magazine stories to gain the experience and confidence to return to novels. In 1902, she published *The Emperor's Candlesticks* in longer form.

Soon after, she wrote *The Scarlet Pimpernel*, which was also rejected. Orczy recast the tale in play form; it was a smash hit, allowing for the novel's successful publication in 1905. Orczy would go on to produce more than twenty Pimpernel sequels over the next thirty-five years, which came to define her legacy. But Orczy wrote a number of other stories, mostly involving espionage, police work, and upper-class heroes -- all recurrent themes in her work.

After 1910, Orczy and her husband moved to Monaco where they lived until World War II. Her husband died in 1942, and Orczy moved to England where she wrote into her 80s.

Biography of Orczy, Emmuska Baroness (1865-1947)

About The Scarlet Pimpernel

The Scarlet Pimpernel was initially rejected by publishers, when Orczy completed it in 1903. Undeterred, she reinvented the book as a play, which went on to be successful, leading to the publication of the book in 1905. The book was an immediate success with the public, relieving Orczy of her financial troubles, but critics found it superficial, classist, and ultimately little more than a disposable lark.

And yet, the public took to the book, looking past its overt sympathies with the noble class, and their demand for more such adventure stories led Orczy to write a slew of Pimpernel sequels over the next forty years. These include *The Laughing Cavalier* (1914), *The First Sir Percy* (1921), *Pimpernel and Rosemary* (1924), and *The Scarlet Pimpernel Looks at the World* (1933).

The Scarlet Pimpernel takes place during the French Revolution, which lasted from 1789-99, and involved an overthrow of the monarchical regime by the peasant classes. This uprising is often seen as a radical manifestation of the egalitarian principles of the Enlightenment. As a result of this uprising, a Reign of Terror took hold, where aristocrats were condemned, imprisoned and sent to the guillotine. In Orczy's novel, a masked hero known as the Scarlet Pimpernel rescues those aristocrats trying to flee the gates of Paris and takes them safely to England, where they enjoy diplomatic immunity from the terror of the masses.

Character List

Percy Blakeney (a.k.a the Scarlet Pimpernel)

Percy Blakeney appears to us first as the maligned husband of Lady Blakeney -- one of the richest, most fashionable men in England, but also a reputed dunce. He is built like a truck, apparently, with big shoulders and muscles, but this only adds to his reputation as a stupid stooge. But Percy is of course secretly the Scarlet Pimpernel who raids the barricades of France to save condemned French aristocrats from the guillotine.

Marguerite St. Just / Lady Blakeney

Lady Blakeney, while living in France as an actress, was famous for her beauty, but even more for her charisma, wit, and intelligence. When she marries Percy Blakeney, no one's quite sure what she's thinking. Since he's considered a dull turkey and she a renowned socialite, the consensus is that she's married down. But she discovers her husband's secret identity and we see her husband's heroism through her eyes.

Chauvelin

Chauvelin, the novel's chief villain, is a French agent who has English diplomacy rights. He is in England looking for the Pimpernel and anyone else who is attempting to rescue French aristocrats. His 'hard-hearted, vengeful' nature contrasts with the dashing Pimpernel.

Armand St. Just

Armand St. Just, Marguerite St. Just's brother, is in cahoots with the Pimpernel. Chauvelin uses Armand to blackmail Marguerite in an attempt to get to the Pimpernel.

Sir Andrew Ffoulkes

Sir Andrew is one of the Scarlet Pimpernel's devoted followers. Marguerite goes to him when she first learns that Percy is the Pimpernel and is thus in danger of being arrested by Chevalier.

Lord Antony Dewhurst

Lord Antony does not last long in the novel, as he is one of the members of the League of the Pimpernel who is captured by Chauvelin at the pub in Dover.

Comtesse de Tournay

The Comtesse is a French aristocrat rescued by the Scarlet Pimpernel in the opening section of the novel, but her husband is left behind, prompting the dramatic rescue that dominates the novel's main plot. She does not like Marguerite

St. Just because she thinks that she caused the demise of the St. Cyr family by denouncing them to the tribunal.

Comte de Tournay

The Comte de Tournay is the Comtesse's husband, rescued from France by the Scarlet Pimpernel.

Lord Grenville

Lord Grenville is an English governmental secretary who holds a grand ball after the opera, a ball which acts as the setting for Chauvelin's and Marguerite's plan to catch the Pimpernel.

Mr. Jellyband

Mr. Jellyband is the propietor of the Dover pub called The Fisherman's Rest, which the Scarlet Pimpernel and his league use for convocations.

Degas

Degas is Chauvelin's most trusted henchman who is sent to retrieve soldiers to arrest the Pimpernel. He consistently arrives too late to trap Percy.

Brogard

Brogard is the pugilistic owner of the Chat Gris inn in Calais where Chauvelin and Percy meet for their face-off.

Marquis de St. Cyr

The Marquis de St. Cyr is a French noble who was condemned because Marguerite made a statement about him to a French tribunal.

Major Themes

Nobility vs. The Masses

When it was first published, The Scarlet Pimpernel was considered classist by critics because it so clearly takes the side of the upper-crust nobles in The French Revolution. Indeed, a key theme that emerges in Orczy's novel is an innate tie between nobility and heroism -- the idea that all the qualities of a grand adventure hero, namely charisma, beauty, elegance, ingenuity, and fashion, are all natural qualities of the noble class. This is, of course, quite obviously wrong (as any look at the actual history that preceded the French Revolution will show), but Orczy, a baroness herself, makes no bones about her allegiance. In order to create sympathy for the nobility, however, she must create the sense that the masses are bloodthirsty enough to kill indiscriminately.

Guilt vs. Redemption

What makes a hero? In Orczy's novel, it's a question often motivated by guilt. Lady Blakeney, for instance, knows that her husband hates her because he thinks she condemned the St. Cyrs to die maliciously; thus she is determined to atone for the sin he thinks she's committed. Meanwhile, Percy seems to feel at least some guilt for deceiving his wife about his identity as the Pimpernel, and enough that he cannot reveal his identity even when she confesses her own internal guilt and turmoil over the St. Cyr incident. Marguerite, meanwhile, has to struggle over the guilt that comes with making the choice between saving her brother, Armand, or saving the Scarlet Pimpernel, who she considers "noble and just." When, of course, it is revealed that the Pimpernel is in fact, her husband, Lady Blakeney is left guilty no matter who she chooses to save. The plot machinations, however, save her from making a choice in the end.

Disguise

The entire scheme of the plot depends on disguise, as The Scarlet Pimpernel wins not through brawn, but rather through cunning and trickery. It's important to remember that given the political context of the novel, the Pimpernel cannot fight fairly. He will be killed by the guillotine if he is merely arrested. Thus disguise as a way of concealing nobility becomes a crucial theme in the novel -- indeed, the Scarlet Pimpernel takes the disguise of people who would be in the masses, including peasants, old hags, old Jews, etc. in order to save the nobility. He is very much a Robin Hood intent on saving the rich, as bizarre as that sounds.

The Scarlet Pimpernel

The flower known as the "the Scarlet Pimpernel" is, according to the narrator, "the name of a humble English wayside flower; but it is also the name chosen to hide the identity of the best and bravest man in all the world." The flower, then, which has become Percy's moniker symbolizes all his best qualities -- his English charm, his humble origins, and his innate humility as a hero that expects no reward for his deeds. Perhaps the most admirable thing about Percy is that he's willing to appear stupid, even buffoonish, in order to secretly continue his missions as the Pimpernel. Indeed, behind a deceptively humble front dwells a hero.

Dual Identities

There is an odd dynamic between England and France that dominates the novel -- the former is depicted as a land of justice and simplicity and order and propriety, whereas the latter is vulnerable to the impulsive rage of mobs and sacrificial violence. As a result, then, Marguerite/Lady Blakeney comes to serve as the perfect symbol of this schism. As Marguerite, she caused the condemnation of the St. Cyr family simply through a misspoken denunciation. Upon marrying Percy Blakeney, she maintains her French casualness -- her haughty charm, but her innate ability to hurt people without thinking. Through the course of the novel, she turns more and more English, evolving gradually into the true Lady Blakeney, who stands by her husband, humble and deferential.

Loyalty

Loyalty becomes a crucial determinant of a person's inherent goodness. Chauvelin maintains his group of loyal henchmen, but their loyalty is based solely on rank, and not to his character. At the end, this superficial loyalty leads to the escape of the fugitives, as Chauvelin's soldiers begrudgingly adhere to his strict instructions, knowing they're letting the prisoners go free -- and yet do not let him know. Meanwhile, Percy's followers put themselves in extreme dangers for the sake of the Pimpernel's cause, because they truly believe in their leader and the plight of the nobility.

Pretension

For all the cult of nobility that surrounds Orczy's novel, she puts a premium on humility. Any character that shows the slightest bit of arrogance or pretension is taught the lesson of humility by the end of the novel. In that, perhaps, Orczy is not so much vindicating nobility as much as instructing a new persona for the "brave, just noble" -- one who fights for the right causes, for humanity instead of riches.

Glossary of Terms

Calais

Calais is the port town across from Dover on the English channel to which travellers arrive when going from England to France. It is where Chauvelin chases Percy after they both flee Dover in search of aristocratic fugitives.

citoyen

Citoyen is the French word for citizen. Various characters are referred to as 'citoyen' by Chauvelin and his other French henchmen.

Comtesse

Comtesse is the French word for Countess. The Comtesse de Tournay, then, is married to a Count, namely the Vicomte de Tournay

Dover

Dover is a small town on the southernmost tip of England. One can cross from Dover to Calais through the narrow Strait of Dover.

Madame de la Guillotine

Madame de la Guillotine is the nickname that the French people gave to the guillotine, an instrument designed for executing people with a huge blade that drops from a pulley to decapitate its victims.

noblesse

Noblesse is the French word for nobility.

Place de la Greve

Place de la Greve is the square in front of the main government building in Paris - where the public guillotine executions were held during the 'Reign of Terror.'

Glossary of Terms

Short Summary

The Scarlet Pimpernel begins in the throes of the French Revolution, with the revolutionary masses at the West Barricade waiting for fleeing aristocrats to be captured and sent to the guillotine. But we learn that in recent times, more and more aristocrats have escaped because of the help of the famous Scarlet Pimpernel who comes in disguise to free the nobility from certain death.

Meanwhile in England, several French escapees gather with the League of The Scarlet Pimpernel in a small pub, where they wait the arrival of the latest refugees. The rescued Comtesse de Tournay soon arrives, with her daughter and son, but says that her husband remains in Paris. She wants to thank the Scarlet Pimpernel for rescuing her, but is told his identity must be kept a secret. She mentions that back in France, the women are terrible for their traitorous actions - and specifically mentions Marguerite St. Just, who condemned a family to die. At that precise moment, Marguerite St. Just arrives.

Here in England, Marguerite St. Just is known as Lady Blakeney, for she is married to Percy Blakeney, the richest and most fashionable man in England. But Percy is also seemingly a buffoon - imbecilic and dull, and when the Comtesse's son challenges him to a duel to avenge his mother's disdain of Marguerite, Percy looks even more the fool as his wife wittily defuses the situation.

Lady Blakeney's brother leaves for France, but before he leaves, he urges his sister to tell Percy why she denounced the St. Cyr family, but she says he already hates her for it, no matter the circumstances. As she goes back to the pub, she meets Chauvelin, a French officer, intent on discovering the identity of the Scarlet Pimpernel. He has been spying on the activities of the Englishmen at the pub, and says that Marguerite must help him find the Pimpernel. She refuses.

Later that night, two members of the League of the Pimpernel are ambushed by Chauvelin just as they discuss plans to rescue the Countess's husband. Chauvelin finds a letter from Marguerite's brother, Armand, and now he sees that he can blackmail her to help her find the Pimpernel.

Chauvelin corners Lady Blakeney at the opera and reveals the letter he has found. If she does not help him, he will ensure that her brother is executed.

At the ball that night, Lady Blakeney finds out that the Pimpernel will be waiting in one of the rooms at one o'clock that night. But when she tells Chauvelin of this, he goes to the room, only to find Percy stretched out on the couch taking a nap. Chauvelin tells Lady Blakeney that she better help him find the Scarlet Pimpernel or else her brother will be in danger.

Lady Blakeney and Percy go to their country home outside the city of London.

Under the stress of all of her dealings with Chauvelin and the coolness of her husband, Lady Blakeney explains the circumstances that led her to denounce the Marquis de Cyr's family at the tribunal. But Percy says she's told him too late and he remains cool to her, even though deep down he still loves her. He promises to save her brother.

Later that night, Lady Blakeney is peeking around her husband's study when she finds a ring emblazoned with the image of the Scarlet Pimpernel -- she discovers his true identity. And indeed, now she realizes she has betrayed her own husband to Chauvelin - and must make the choice between saving him and her brother.

Lady Blakeney sails to Calais, where she hides at an inn, only to witness a tense encounter between Percy and Chauvelin, who have accidentally run into each other. Unbeknownst to Percy, however, Chauvelin has six soldiers on the way to arrest him.

But Percy manages to outwit Chauvelin and he escapes, and a chase ensues to find him. Marguerite follows behind as Chauvelin and his henchmen enlist the help of an Old Jew, who claims to know the way that Percy left.

The Jew takes them to a hut, where Marguerite realizes that the fugitives are hiding. She throws herself towards the hut in an effort to save the ones inside, but she's captured by Chauvelin. Chauvelin and his henchmen go inside the hunt and find that its empty. A moment later they see a boat drifting out of the harbor and realize the fugitives have escaped.

Chauvelin leads his men on a hunt for Percy, but not after making sure the old Jew is mercilessly beaten. Only after Chauvelin leaves does the old Jew get up groggily and reveals himself to the bound Marguerite as her husband Percy in disguise.

Percy and Marguerite set sail for England the next day, reconciled, having freed the fugitives and Percy promises to make sure Chauvelin never steps foot in English noble society again.

Summary and Analysis of Chapters 1-4

Summary

Orczy plunges us into the throes of the French revolution, as "a surging, seething, murmuring crowd of beings that are human only in name," gathers at Paris' West Barricade. During the day, these masses watch hundreds of aristocrats lose their heads at the guillotine, condemned as 'traitors' to France. In the afternoon, they gather at the gates of the city to watch the daily attempts of the aristocrats to evade Sargent Bibot.

Though Bibot has had great success in preventing aristocrats from leaving the city, recently a large number have succeeded in escaping France and reaching England safely. The rumor is that a band of Englishmen have taken to helping the aristocrats escape -- leaving behind the sign of a star-shaped flower, the scarlet pimpernel, as a marker.

Bibot scrutinizes a passing cart for hidden aristocrats, but quickly lets them go when the old hag driver tells him that her grandson has small-pox. Soon enough, Bibot realizes his mistake when a captain comes bounding up -- for the old hag was the 'accursed Englishman himself -- the Scarlet Pimpernel.'

The setting moves to a small pub in Dover called The Fisherman's Rest. Here, English men and women await several French aristocrats who have managed to escape from Paris with the help of the Scarlet Pimpernel. Two of these Englishmen, Lord Antony Dewhurst and Sir Andrew Ffoulkes, close accomplices of The Scarlet Pimpernel.

The Comtesse de Tournay soon arrives with her daughter and son, lamenting that her husband remains in Paris while she has escaped with her children. She prays for his successful rescue and asks whether she can meet the Scarlet Pimpernel, the man who has saved her and her children's life. She is told it is impossible, for the Pimpernel's identity is strictly secret.

The Comtesse recounts her terrifying experience crossing through the barricades with the old hag in the driver's seat, expecting to be found out at any moment. She mentions that the women in France have been especially cooperative in executing aristocrats. The Comtesse specifically accuses Marguerite St. Just of denouncing a whole family to the tribunal. She mentions that she heard Marguerite St. Just married an Englishman and hopes aloud that she never sees her again.

But her hosts feel terribly awkward, for Marguerite St. Just, having married an Englishman, is now Lady Blakeney. At that precise moment, the Blakeneys arrive outside in their carriage.

Analysis

From the outset, *The Scarlet Pimpernel* makes no secret of its genre -- it's a swashbuckling adventure devoid of subtlety. The book careens from location to location, telling a story of heroism and nobility, all while maintaining a tense plot. The wonder of Orczy's novel is its economy and pacing; no sooner is a character mentioned, such as the Comtesse de Tournay, than that character appears. This approach, though lacking in subtlety, maximizes plot twists and suspense. As we look at The Scarlet Pimpernel, its crucial that we consider structure as the most crucial element in the book; no matter how endearing the characters, if the plot couldn't sustain momentum and economy, the novel would collapse. The melodrama of the story only works when abetted by an unceasing storyline full of action and plot twists.

The opening resonates with myth -- it presents no characters that we'll see again, simply telling the legend of the Pimpernel who would free those aristocrats condemned to die. Orczy thus pulls off a nifty trick: the natural sympathies of the reader would be expected to be with the masses against the aristocrats, but by telling the legend of the Pimpernel, presenting him straightaway and unambiguously as the hero, Orczy encourages us to feel awe and admiration for the man who would rescue these doomed aristocrats. Though the reader is more likely to be a member of the "masses" than the nobility, the mythic presentation of the Pimpernel does not allow us to identify with the forces of democracy.

The Comtesse de Tournay's arrival is odd; though we certainly expect her to be a pivotal character, she soon falls away dramatically, not really to return again. Indeed, when she faces off against Lady Blakeney, we take the Comtesse's side -- believing her story that Marguerite St. Just had condemned the St. Cyr family to die. But slowly, as we're immersed into this world of nobility, we start to realize that the masses are not our protagonists at all, that "Orczy's sympathy with the deposed nobility and old order is evident" (Brantley, xi).

Moreover, Lady Blakeney's seeming haughtiness makes us wonder whether she is to be a villain. Orczy's descriptions of Lady Blakeney consistently mention her beauty, charm, wit, and other priceless virtues, but as the reader, we have a harder time seeing these positive qualities in action. The nature of sympathy for Lady Blakeney is a key analytical point we will continue to track as we continue, but for now, it's important to note that we do not necessarily see her as our novel's heroine.

For the most part, however, these opening chapters are principally about exposition - the nature of the conflict in the revolution between the masses and the 'traitorous' aristocrats, the rescue of the Comtesse but the remainder of her husband behind, the league of the Scarlet Pimpernel and his mysterious identity, and the seemingly duplicitous nature of Lady Blakeney. When the Blakeneys arrive, we are fully ready for the beginning of our adventure, but quite unsure as to who is our protagonist.

Summary and Analysis of Chapters 5-8

Summary

Lady Blakeney arrives, despite the Comtesse's refusal to see her. Indeed, the Comtesse makes a grand gesture of forbidding her daughter from speaking to Lady Blakeney. The Comtesse leaves with her daughter in tow and Lady Blakeney reveals her haughtiness, mocking the Comtesse afterwards.

Yet there's a crucial moment where we see the 'hard, set expression vanish, and a wistful, almost pathetic and childlike look steal' into Lady Blakeney's eyes. In this moment we see that Lady Blakeney is not nearly as haughty or unfeeling as she might seem.

Her husband Percy Blakeney arrives. He is one of the richest men in England, 'leader of all fashions,' and managed to secure 'a brilliant matrimonial prize' in Lady Blakeney, a 'beautiful, fascinating, clever, French wife' who had many suitors. But Percy himself seems terribly dull -- even stupid. The narrator comments that society wonders how he managed to woo Lady Blakeney.

As the Comtesse has insulted Lady Blakeney, the Comtesse's son emerges to challenge Percy to a duel to allow Percy to settle the score. But Lady Blakeney is so effective in her shrill mocking of the men -- both her husband and the Comtesse's son -- that the duel is avoided.

Percy, meanwhile, is an almost cartoonish fop, clearly intimidated by his wife, Lady Blakeney, and puerile in his language. But as Lady Blakeney leaves, the narrator remarks on the deep intense look in Percy's eyes as he watches her, a sign of complexity in Percy that we hang on to.

Outside, Lady Blakeney wishes her brother Armand farewell, before he returns to France to continue serving the country. Armand asks whether Lady Blakeney has told her husband of the full circumstances of her denunciation of the Marquis de Cyr's family to the tribunal -- circumstances which apparently exonerate her from all blame. But Lady Blakeney says she has not, and as a result, her relationship with her husband has been destroyed.

As Marguerite goes back to the pub, she meets Chauvelin, a French officer who is intent on discovering the identity of the Scarlet Pimpernel. He has been spying on the activities of the Englishmen at the pub, and says that Marguerite must help him find the Pimpernel. She refuses, saying he is a brave and noble man, and she would never lend a hand to assist in his capture.

Analysis

By the end of these chapters, Lady Blakeney has evolved into our chief protagonist, but it's an uneasy role for her, because as the reader we're not convinced that she warrants our sympathies. We begin to soften towards her in the key scene where she converses with her brother, Armand St. Just. Armand urges Lady Blakeney to reveal the circumstances which led to her condemnation of St. Cyr's family -- circumstances which would appease those who doubt her innocence. But Lady Blakeney reveals that its too late -- Percy already hates her.

This exchange, where Lady Blakeney reveals her husband's secret contempt for her, is one of the most compelling in the novel: it reveals different themes that will evolve in the course of the story. First, it reveals that Lady Blakeney respects her husband's opinion despite earlier giving the impression that he's a useless dimwit; we understand that she gives him far more credit in private than she does in public. Second, it reveals that Percy has a deeper side to him, for in the earlier scene, he seems not only incapable of feeling, but boorish and dull as well. Third, and perhaps most importantly, it reveals Percy's deep allegiance to the League of the Scarlet Pimpernel. For him to hate his wife so deeply over her denunciation of the St. Cyr family reveals Percy's profound commitment to the Pimpernel's cause. He feels more deeply for the St. Cyr's than he does for his own beautiful and popular wife -- an interesting character wrinkle that straight-off should give us a clue as to Percy's true identity.

Already, many of the characters in *The Scarlet Pimpernel* appear to be "red herrings"; they vie for our sympathies only to fade into the background as unimportant. The Comtesse de Tournay, though a central figure in the first chapters, does not have a significant role in the book. Her ultimate importance is as a foil: she allows us to wonder about Lady Blakeney's innocence and introduces the major plot movement of the book, the rescue of the Comtesse's husband.

But the biggest red herring in the book is seemingly Seargent Bibot, who is placed squarely at the outset as our villain. We fully expect Bibot to be the foil to the Pimpernel and a classic battle between them to ultimately provide our climax. But Bibot never returns; instead, he is replaced in Chapter Eight by Chauvelin, a Frenchman on a mission to capture the Pimpernel. It's an odd choice by Orczy, for we're disoriented by Chauvelin's appearance -- and aren't quite sure whether he's our *real* villain, or simply a shadowy stand-in for a larger force. In time we'll come to see him as the villain of the book, but for now, we're still uneasy with our hierarchy of characters, with neither a clear hero nor antagonist.

Additionally, it's important to note that many of the key moments in the book come from our omniscient narrator, who offers insights that we can't divest from the action of the plot. In particular, we believe Lady Blakeney is haughty, and Percy is dull, but the narrator finds the pitiful, childlike expression in Lady Blakeney as the Comtesse leaves, and the intense depth in Percy's look as his wife leaves. Indeed, without the narrator, we're not quite sure what to feel of these characters. With the narrator's help, we glean hints as to the character's interior secrets, foreshadowing the revelations to come.

Analysis

Summary and Analysis of Chapters 9-14

Summary

Back at the pub, later in the night, two of the Englishmen talk of the need for the Pimpernel to return to France immediately to save the Comtesse's husband, the Comte de Tournay, who has been sentenced to death. But as they begin to read the Pimpernel's instructions for moving forward, they are ambushed by Chauvelin's men. Chauvelin scours the room for evidence and finds a letter signed by Lady Blakeney's brother, Armand. He leaves satisfied, knowing he now has a way to blackmail Lady Blakeney into helping him find the Scarlet Pimpernel.

At Covent Garden Theater, the Comtesse de Tournay attends the opera, only to be reminded of the continuing horrors in France and the unlikelihood that her husband will make it out alive. She remarks bitterly that should Chauvelin need an accomplice, he should seek out Lady Blakeney.

Chauvelin corners Lady Blakeney at the opera and reveals the letter he has found. If she does not help him, he will ensure that her brother is executed. He tells her that if she helps him at Lord Grenville's Ball to discover the identity of the Pimpernel, who is supposed to be meeting with his men in secret during the course of the party, then he will give her her brother's letter the next day, and she can destroy it.

At the ball, Lady Blakeney is paralyzed with anxiety, fearing for her brother's life. She can't explain the situation to her husband, Percy, who she finds completely useless, and thus believes she must shoulder the situation alone. She follows two of the Englishmen and sees them hand-off a note. She follows the man who has the note to a room, where she distracts him long enough to read it just before he sets it to flame. The note says that the Scarlet Pimpernel will be in the supper room at one o'clock.

Lady Blakeney tells Chauvelin what she has read in the note. He goes to the supper room, only to find Percy Blakeney napping on the sofa in the corner. Chauvelin stretches out on a couch as well, waiting for the Pimpernel to appear. He doesn't, and Chauvelin tells Marguerite that she better hope that the Pimpernel is caught: her brother is not saved yet.

Analysis

Chauvelin becomes a real villain when he orchestrates an ambush on the league of the Scarlet Pimpernel, but he's a complex villain in that he doesn't seem innately evil or cruel. The adventure genre makes a staple of the abnormally brutal or deviant villain (often with a scar) who butchers victims, increases the body count, and preys on our fears, so that when he finally meets the hero in a climactic encounter, we fear not just the hero's death, but his suffering.

Meanwhile, Chauvelin seems a bit of a mouse. We aren't particularly afraid of him personally -- but what we are afraid of is his power, for he has the office to send any aristocrat to the guillotine of the revolutionary mob. And as the reader, it is the guillotine that we fear, not any individual combat between hero and villain.

Chauvelin presents the initial plot crisis with the revelation that Armand is part of the League of the Scarlet Pimpernel. This single letter provides the impetus for all that is to follow - for now Lady Blakeney has her own sympathies torn, between saving her brother and betraying the Pimpernel. But whereas Percy chooses the Pimpernel over blood, Lady Blakeney chooses blood over allegiance to the hero and tells Chauvelin she'll help him find the stealthy Englishman.

Orczy pulls off the best sequence of the novel in the run-up to the secret meeting between the Pimpernel and his followers at Lord Grenville's ball. For when we arrive at the secret meeting room, through the eyes of Chauvelin, only to find Percy, we as the reader fall for the trap, believing Percy an innocent bystander. Certainly the clues have already been laid for us to feel foolish when it is revealed that Percy is the Pimpernel, but she uses three main devices to distract us -- the omniscient narrator, who we've so far trusted as representing the truth, but who now happily misleads us by using the filters of Chauvelin's point of view; the failure of Lady Blakeney to take her husband seriously; and the consistent build-up of the revelation of the Pimpernel, as if he is to be a new character that can finally take the place of protagonist.

That said, it is clear now that Lady Blakeney is the emotional center of the novel, for more and more Orczy's narrator takes times to examine her torn feelings. If there is a fault to the storytelling in *The Scarlet Pimpernel*, it is Lady Blakeney's failure as the protagonist to truly drive the action. More and more as the novel progresses, we are privileged to Blakeley's interior thoughts; however, she merely responds to her torn allegiances, wallowing in the difficulty of her position without doing anything about it.

Summary and Analysis of Chapters 15-19

Summary

Lady Blakeney and Percy go to their country home outside the city of London. Under the stress of all of her dealings with Chauvelin and the coolness of her husband, Lady Blakeney explains the circumstances that led her to denounce the Marquis de Cyr's family at the tribunal -- namely that she was tricked into the condemnation.

Percy isn't sympathetic. He tells her that she should have revealed her role earlier. Lady Blakeney asks for her husband's help in saving her brother but Percy remains cold. He says that perhaps she should ask Armand, but Lady Blakeney isn't sure how to tell him that she needs her husband's help, since it's Chauvelin who is blackmailing her.

Still, Percy perceives his wife's fear and assures her that her brother will be safe -- though he still withholds even the slightest sign of affection. Lady Blakeney fears that she has lost her husband's love for good. Only when Lady Blakeney leaves, despondent by her husband's refusal to show her love, do we see Percy break down, clearly still very much in love with his wife.

Lady Blakeney realizes she has always been in love with Percy and that she has underestimated him. The next day she finds Percy about to leave for the North, and is surprised by his mysterious departure. And yet she feels confident that it has something to do with his promise to save her brother.

Lady Blakeney takes the opportunity of Percy's absence to peak into his study, which is organized and neat. She wonders why Percy presents the image of the buffoon, when he is clearly a competent and thoughtful man. She sees a small gold ring on the carpet, which she picks up. It has a flat shield, engraved with a scarlet pimpernel. Lady Blakeney suddenly realizes the true identity of her husband.

Indeed, not only does she realize her husband's true identity, but Lady Blakeney also realizes that she has unwittingly betrayed him to Chauvelin, who plans on intercepting the Pimpernel in Calais. Soon a messenger arrives carrying her brother's letter -- which Lady Blakeney takes as evidence that Chauvelin is close to catching the Scarlet Pimpernel.

Analysis

This stretch of chapters is primarily about the relationship between Lady Blakeney and Percy, which deepens the complexity of our two central characters just before the key revelation of Percy's secret identity. It's curious, of course, that *The Scarlet Pimpernel* is nearly half over before we know our hero, for we never really see the enigmatic rescuer in action until after Percy is revealed to be the Pimpernel. In this light, the book seems to be a romance masquerading as an adventure, more a story of a broken marriage mended by the revelation of heroism in both husband and wife.

When Lady Blakeney tries to confess to Percy the circumstances of her denunciation of the St. Cyr family to the tribunal, Percy is uncharacteristically cold. For the first time his mask of buffoonery drops, and we see him as a man capable of feeling and depth. Indeed, when he tells his wife that he will ensure Armand's safety, we not only believe him, but begin to suspect that he has a dual nature -- one that justifies his level of intensity.

That said, Percy still does not take over the role of hero here. We remain in Lady Blakeney's point of view, confused as to his sudden disappearance, confused as to his identity until she finds the ring in his study. Percy is less an adventure hero and more a romantic one; we see him through the eyes of his beloved, and regaining love appears to be the primary goal of the story, rather than the rescue of parties in danger. Before the "adventure" story can properly begin, we first address the "tragic romance" story. With Percy's worthiness and identity established, Orczy finally sets about giving her audience the adventure they've been expecting.

Structurally, it is important that we note the use of "hooks" at the end of each chapter, especially as we delve into the action-adventure portion of the novel. *The Scarlet Pimpernel* is not so unlike a TV serial or a serialized novel in that it depends on the suspense of the final sentence or paragraph in order to raise the reader's adrenaline and expectations in advance of the next section. For instance, later in the book, we'll hear Percy sing "God save the King!" to announce his arrival at key moments, an action that makes zero sense since he's attempting to *hide* from the authorities, but one which builds suspense for the reader. Thus, at the end of this section, when Lady Blakeney finds the Scarlet Pimpernel ring, it is a terribly convenient discovery -- a coincidence that might even lead a reader to groan -- but one that works well as an end-of-chapter hook.

Analysis

Summary and Analysis of Chapters 20-24

Summary

Lady Blakeney goes to see Sir Andrew, a friend of the Pimpernel, and reveals the trap -- that she has unwittingly betrayed Percy, who she knows to be the Pimpernel, and he is now on his way into the hands of Chauvelin at Calais. Though Andrew tries to convince Lady Blakeney to leave affairs in his hands, she insists on going with him. They plot to meet that night in Dover to sail for Calais the next day.

Andrew arrives and tells Lady Blakeney that no one will sail from Dover that night because of the strong storm. Andrew suggests just killing Chauvelin in order to end the matter, but Lady Blakeney tells him that the penalties for capture of murderers is too high a price to pay. They spend the night at the pub, waiting for the storm to pass.

The side-effect of the storm is that Chauvelin no longer has his head start on Lady Blakeney and the Englishmen. Indeed, now when the storm passes, she will have the upper hand, provided she can find Percy before he runs into Chauvelin. Moreover, should Chauvelin see her there, he would suspect her involvement in aiding Percy and the other fugitives from France.

The next day they sail to Calais, where they go to the Chat Gris, a small pub, and discover that the master of the inn, named Brogard, expects Percy to return that evening for supper. Lady Blakeney is overjoyed, but realized that now they are on French soil: if Percy were to be apprehended, his fate would quickly be sealed.

At the same time, Andrew reminds Lady Blakeney why Percy came to Calais -- namely to free the Count de Tournay, as well as her brother. Lady Blakeney realizes that there is no way that Percy would leave without the fugitives, and she grants that Andrew must find Percy and warn him about Chauvelin's hunt. Meanwhile, Lady Blakeney will hide in the Chat Gris should Percy return for supper, but Andrew instructs her not to reveal herself to him.

Marguerite waits at the inn for Percy and soon enough a man arrives. But it is Chauvelin. She listens as Chauvelin instructs his henchman, Degas, to return with six soldiers and ambush Percy the moment he walks into the pub. But he says that he wants Percy "alive... if possible." Degas leaves, and Chauvelin waits for him to return.

Lady Blakeney is horrified at the obvious danger her husband faces. She sees that despite his heroism, her husband will be no match for Chauvelin's soldiers. Thus Lady Blakeney waits in despair -- and indeed, soon enough she hears Percy's voice outside singing lustily as he approaches.

Analysis

In perhaps the oddest section of Orczy's novel, Lady Blakeney is rendered a suddenly passive, almost immobile character. Indeed, though she has grown increasingly emotional fragile as the novel progresses, she has at least been a figure of action, driving the plot onward. In these sections, however, the only action Lady Blakeney takes is to beg for help from supporting characters whom we know little of. Otherwise, she spends her time... waiting.

In what has to be one of the most bizarre plot choices of the book, Orczy chooses to stop the momentum completely by using a storm to abort the race between Lady Blakeney and Chauvelin to Calais. For nearly two chapters, we wait while Marguerite sits at the pub, drowning in her own fear and anxiety, simply waiting for the chapter to end and her trip to begin the next day. On an plot level, we can chalk up this device to Orczy's wish to have Marguerite reach Calais before Chauvelin, eliminating Chauvelin's head-start; but it is a rather clumsy, even lazy choice of tactics, for it slows our pacing in this crucial stretch of the novel -- and indeed distances us further from Percy.

Of Percy, meanwhile, we are nearly at the end of the book and know little to nothing of his heroism. What is so striking about *The Scarlet Pimpernel* in its depiction of heroism is its refusal to ever take us inside the hero's point of view. We are always left to admire the results of his action, the objective sequences of events, rather than witness the thoughts, strategy, or interior conflicts that bears them out. In that, there is an odd dynamic between the masculine and feminine here, as Marguerite's point-of-view remains fairly passive -- she is merciless at the hands of men, who we never fully understand, but admire for their nobility and bravery.

To take this a step farther, as the genre of *The Scarlet Pimpernel* shifts from romance to adventure, the emphasis shifts from the feminine action of Lady Blakeney to the secret masculine action of the Pimpernel. As long as the focus of the novel is on the struggles of marriage, Lady Blakeney emerges as a complicated, deep, interesting woman. When it comes to action, however, she is reduced to a hapless "damsel in distress," a mere witness to the Pimpernel's heroism.

Chauvelin becomes more threatening once he's on French soil in Calais. When he tells Degas to return with his soldiers, we begin to understand just how much danger Percy is actually in. Indeed, it is not Percy's death at the hands of Chauvelin that we fear, but his simple arrest -- for that ensures his execution at the hands of the masses and guillotine. Therefore Percy's margin for error is much smaller -- he can not win in a hand-to-hand climax with Chauvelin; he cannot succeed simply through brawn and physical prowess. Rather the victory here must be about rescue and physical escape without allowing a face-to-face meeting.

Thus when Percy arrives at the Chat Gris in the last line "hook" of the chapter, the reader realizes both the inherent danger of the situation and also the additional fear that comes with the filter of Marguerite's defenseless point-of-view. We will watch Percy for the very first time as the Scarlet Pimpernel, and though we may not be privy to his thoughts or feelings, at the very least we'll have first-hand observation of why he deserves to be our hero.

Summary and Analysis of Chapters 25-28

Summary

The meeting between Chauvelin and Percy is understandably awkward, and Chauvelin realizes he needs time before Degas returns with the men to arrest Blakeney. Meanwhile, Lady Blakeney watches from the stairwell, horrified. Percy, nonplussed, eats his dinner, and asks Chauvelin trivial questions; the Frenchman gets ever more eager for his henchmen to arrive.

Percy innocently asks Chauvelin if he would like to inhale a top-notch brand of snuff he acquired from abroad. Chauvelin falls for the trap, ends up inhaling pepper, and Percy calmly leaves the room as Chauvelin struggles -- just before the soldiers arrive.

The soldiers tell Chauvelin that they found out Percy had talked to a Jew named Reuben about borrowing his horse and cart later that night to go down the St. Martin road. Chauvelin demands that they find Reuben, but they can't find him and instead bring a fellow old Jew who claims to be a friend of his.

The Jew says that he can lend the soldiers his horse and cart and they will go to Pere Blanchard's hut, where Percy is to supposed to end his ride on Reuben's horse. The Jew claims that the horse that Percy took is a miserable nag who can't move at more than a snail's place. Since the Jew claims his horse is faster than Reuben's, he said Chauvelin will either catch up with Percy or get to the Pere Blanchard hut before Percy gets there.

Chauvelin decides to trust the Jew, but makes a very clear deal. If they catch up with Percy, he will offer the Jew a monetary reward. But if they do not, he will make sure that the Jew is beaten mercilessly, even to death. The arrangement is confirmed and the Jew provides his nag to help the soldiers catch up with Percy.

Lady Blakeney leaves her hiding spot and eavesdrops as soldiers tell Chauvelin that Percy has not been found along the road to Pere Blanchard's hut. Chauvelin tells them not to attack Percy until they find the other fugitives that he is rescuing as well. All of them arrive at the hut, and Chauvelin decides to take the old Jew with him so that he doesn't make noise and mistakenly warn the Scarlet Pimpernel that he is walking into a trap.

When the light of the moon illuminates the area around the hut, Lady Blakeney sees Percy's ship anchored beneath the cliffs. Realizing that Percy is here, about to walk into the trap, she runs towards Pere Blanchard's hut to warn the people inside, but she's captured by Chauvelin.

Analysis

Percy's evolution into the swashbuckling hero, courtesy of a new focus on him as the protagonist, finds assistance in Chauvelin's gross incompetence. Indeed, Chauvelin becomes increasingly idiotic with each new scene. For instance, when Percy arrives and sits down to a calm supper, despite Chauveline's presence, it is Chauvelin's fear that we feel through the subtext, rather than Percy's. Maguerite may be afraid for Percy, but he displays such command that we do not doubt for an instant his impending escape.

It's a curious choice to make the hero so devoid of inner conflict and transparency; the Scarlet Pimpernel appears to have no discernible motivation, no depths or complexities apart from the superficial problem of his "secret" identity. He's as two-dimensional as a comic book character -- and, indeed, the Scarlet Pimpernel is widely considered the forerunner to the pulp action comic heroes of the twenties and thirties. This lack of depth succeeds because Orczy narratorial maintains the point-of-view of an awed spectator and uses Marguerite as Percy's emotional anchor. As long as she's in fear of what's to happen, we'll fear for Percy's life -- even if he himself has no doubts about his escape.

Chauvelin ludicrous impulse to accept snuff from Percy is, of course, remarkably convenient -- and quite juvenile -- as a plot device, but we accept it if only to keep the plot moving. The escape also emasculates Chauvelin and puts an even higher premium on Percy's cleverness. If he does not dazzle us with cunning and ingenious means of escape, we will lose interest -- for we certainly do not see Chauvelin as a worthy match.

Critics have pointed to the obvious prejudice in the delineation of the Jew character, and with good reason. That said, characterization in the novel is typically broad, and the later revelation that Percy himself is the Jew softens the depiction somewhat. Still, not giving the character a proper name, and referring to him only as 'The Jew' adds to the classism of the novel as a whole. A reader ought to keep it continually in mind that the subtext of *The Scarlet Pimpernel* is the worthiness of the aristocracy and the "old ways" of life -- ways which include racism, classism, and undisguised distaste for the masses.

Geography is a bit confusing here, and we have the slight suspicion its because Orczy is trying to keep the pace quick enough to distract us from some of the implausibilities of the actual chase. Indeed, we're never quite sure how Lady Blakeney keeps up with the parties and manages to be in all the right places at the right times, but for now, we take these chapters as more intermediate steps of exposition in order to get our principal characters -- Percy, Chauvelin, and Marguerite -- to Pere Blanchard's hut. It is a testament to Orczy's characterization of Marguerite that we are invested fully in her desire to save Percy now -- so we follow her exclusively and worry little about the details of how everyone will arrive at Pere Blanchard's hut.

What's slightly ironic is for all of Marguerite's fears of having to choose between Percy and Armand, she ultimately doesn't have to make that choice. (Indeed, as the novel fully embraces its swashbuckling nature, the complexities that have crept into the narrative are neatly ironed away.) Once she sees the Daydreamer boat anchored in the bay, she realizes she must save both at once, and goes hurtling towards the hut in her first decisive action in many, many chapters. Finally, our heroine has emerged -- only to be captured by Chauvelin, hence revealing Marguerite as the weakest of our principal characters. Her role, once defined by complicated choices and hidden depths, has devolved to become another mere foil for The Pimpernel's heroics.

Analysis

Summary and Analysis of Chapters 29-31

Summary

Lady Blakeney comes to, realizing she is outside the hut with Chauvelin and his soldiers just as they're waiting to ambush those waiting inside. Chauvelin tells her that she must remain silent if she wants her brother to remain alive. Lady Blakeney doesn't know what to do -- whether to save her brother or Percy -- but just then she hears Percy's voice singing 'God save the King!' out in the distance.

Lady Blakeney cannot stay silent and screams; she runs to the hut and shouts for those inside to save themselves. The soldiers grab her, run into the hut but it is empty. By following Chauvelin's strict orders -- to stand guard outside, waiting for Percy before doing anything with the fugitives -- they unwittingly let the fugitives free. Chauvelin promises his henchmen that they will die for their mistake, but they let Chauvelin know that they didn't go after the escaping fugitives in deference to his orders.

But suddenly down below the cliffs, they hear gunfire from the anchored boat. The fugitives have escaped onto the boat, and it sets sail for England. Chauvelin despairs momentarily before he realizes that he heard Percy's singing -- and that Percy must still be in the vicinity.

He finds a letter in the hut that tells the fugitives to go without him as he'll be near a creak outside the Chat Gris. Chauvelin sends his soldiers to find Percy -- but before he leaves, realizes that the Jew has been left unpunished. He tells his soldiers to bring the Jew.

He tells the Jew that the deal they made was clear -- and that not only did his horse fail to overtake Percy's, but that now even the fugitives have gone free. He orders his soldiers to beat the Jew mercilessly, which they do while Chauvelin watches and Marguerite lays unconscious.

Later, Marguerite awakes to hear the beaten Jew cursing -- in a clearly British accent. She runs to him to find that the Jew is indeed Percy in disguise. She frees him, they rejoice over his cunning, impenetrable scheme, and indeed, as the final part of his plan, Sir Andrew arrives, having followed his orders, to take them both to the returning boat, which soon sets sail for their home in England.

The novel ends with the resolution of both plot strands -- the reconciliation of husband and wife and the restoration of confidence between them, and the freedom of the remaining fugitives from the terror of the French revolutionary masses.

Analysis

The climax and denouement of *The Scarlet Pimpernel* surprisingly is devoid of any physical combat or face-to-face action. Indeed, more than an adventure novel, we seem to have wandered into the espionage genre, where the goal is to evade, conceal, and ambush rather than embrace man-to-man combat. Furthermore, just as the end of each chapter in Orczy's novel relies on the dangling hook, the final machinations of the plot depend on the creativity and uniqueness of Percy's stratagems. We fully expect his escape -- but the question is whether we can predict or anticipate the nature of his plans.

For all her seemingly heroic plans at the end of the novel -- twice she tries to save Percy and the fugitives -- Marguerite is again rendered helpless and useless:

"The cleverest woman in Europe, the elegant and fashionable Lady Blakeney, who had dazzled London society with her beauty, her wit and her extravagances, presented a very pathetic picture of tired-out, suffering womanhood, which would have appealed to any, but hard, vengeful heart of her baffled enemy."

It's a curious passage, because our heroine is left so "pathetic" and pitiable. There is made a clear distinction here between man and woman, with the latter incapable and doomed to futility. It's a romantic vision of womanhood, and one that could potentially work, except for the fact that we don't especially feel threatened by Chauvelin's "hard, vengeful heart." Indeed, we're not quite sure what Chauvelin's motivation is, whether it's lust for Lady Blakeney (doubtful), desire to rise in rank and position (not really evident), or just hard-hearted evil (not borne out by the text). So Orczy's narrator, in her explanation of Chauvelin as the bearer of a "hard, vengeful heart," isn't particularly convincing.

The ending of the novel resolves both of our primary conflicts -- as husband and wife reconcile, primarily with Lady Blakeney in awe of Percy's cleverness, completing his character's arc from seeming buffoon to ingenious swashbuckler. Moreover, the fugitives are freed, which truly prevents any climactic showdown where Marguerite would have had to choose between Percy and her brother.

The final moments have a fairy tale absurdity. Percy manages to get into new, fashionable clothes on his boat, clothes "of which he always kept a supply on board his yacht." Marguerite finds a pair of shoes so "she could put foot on English shore in his best pair," and the rest is "silence" -- the silence of a perfect ending where everyone gets their happily ever after. Indeed, the close of the book is a firm reminder that this, after all, is melodrama at its most self-indulgent -- a slight fairy tale meant to divert and entertain, a bit of revisionist mythology set in a dreadful historical moment. Finally the nobility get their very own Robin Hood.

But we should not allow this fun, frivolous conclusion to overwhelm the clear class signals of the novel. The Baroness Orczy was herself, after all, a deposed aristocrat;

her simple celebration of the aristocracy of France, which totally ignores the excesses and injustices that sparked the French Revolution in the first place, seems at the last reckoning to be a personal fantasy, with the naturally clever and resourceful aristocrats outwitting the flat-footed masses. *The Scarlet Pimpernel* is a deceptively complicated book: a celebration of individual heroism with a subtext that endorses traditionalism and conservatism; a simple, contrived yarn with passages of psychological subtlety (and the overarching psychology of the author); a revenge fantasy of the aristocracy in an increasingly democratic Europe. It's ironic, then, that the very masses whom the book scorns -- the book-buying, romance-reading masses -- ensured that *The Scarlet Pimpernel* is a perennial bestseller.

Suggested Essay Questions

1. Do you consider the narrator to be impartial? Does the narrator ally him or herself with a class, a country, a cause?
2. Who is the central protagonist in *The Scarlet Pimpernel*? In other words, who carries the emotional weight of the novel?
3. How is point-of-view a crucial device in the rendering of Percy? Do we ever experience events through his perspective? How is his heroism dependent upon the way he is seen?
4. At what point does Lady Blakeney become a sympathetic character? Would you consider her an unlikable character as she initially appears?
5. What purpose does the Comtesse de Tournay serve in the larger arc of the novel? Why do you think she disappears after the first section of the book?
6. How does Chauvelin manage to be a threatening villain without ever having to engage in physical combat with the Pimpernel? Is he ultimately threatening?
7. How is the Scarlet Pimpernel flower a larger motif for the themes of the novel? Does it fit Percy as a character?
8. Why doesn't Chauvelin have to die at the end of the book for a successful resolution? Would the novel have been more satisfying with a different resolution, or does the resolution as Orczy presents it fit the tenor of the book as a whole?
9. How does loyalty play a key role in the distinction between Percy succeeding and Chauvelin failing in achieving their goals? Are these respective men's followers equally loyal to their causes? Is their loyalty distinct?
10. Is Percy a less admirable hero for never physically taking on his enemies? What is his ultimate goal as the Scarlet Pimpernel?

Suggested Essay Questions

The History of the Guillotine

Perhaps more than any other single cause, it is the guillotine which inspired the term Reign of Terror, coined to capture the fear which infected revolutionary France from 1792 to 1794.

The nobility and monarchy, in losing their power to the revolutionary mob, also became prey to the Revolutionary Tribunal, led by Robespierre, which not only sentenced legions of aristocrats to beheading by the guillotine, but also ensured that these executions would be public. The fear inspired by the guillotine was legendary (indeed, it has came to be nicknamed 'Madame Guillotine'), but more than the fear of the actual mechanics of the death instrument was the fact that little to no evidence was needed to sentence one to death by it. As long as Robiespierre's tribunal offered the charge of 'Crimes Against Liberty,' then a death sentence was practically written in stone.

The Guillotine, as stated in the Pimpernel, took place in a square called La Place de la revolution. Before the Guillotine, the government used to execute people by breaking them on the wheel (an even more cruel and unusual capital punishment device), but deemed inhumane, the National Assembly instilled the use of the Guillotine after commissioning an instrument of execution whose principal charge would be to simply end life, as opposed to inflict pain. Moreover, because of the guillotine's efficiency, it meant that it could be used for the execution of all classes.

The guillotine itself involves a large, massive blade suspended from a rope on a tall frame, so that the impact severs the head from a body in a swift blow. Many observers at the time of execution claimed that the guillotine didn't end life as swiftly as it promised to -- and that the severed heads blinked and made expressions. Science has yet to prove the validity of these claims.

The History of the Guillotine

Author of ClassicNote and Sources

Soman Chainani, author of ClassicNote. Completed on May 05, 2007, copyright held by GradeSaver.

Updated and revised W.C. Miller June 05, 2007. Copyright held by GradeSaver.

Margaret Brantley. The Scarlet Pimpernel: Enriched Edition. New York: Pocket Books, 2004.

Orczy, Baronness. Scarlet Pimpernel: Collector's Edition. London: Dalmatian Press, 2004.

"The Scarlet Pimpernel." 2007-05-04.
<http://www.stpetersnottingham.org/misc/pimpernel.html>.

"Blakeney Manor." 2007-05-04. <http://www.blakeneymanor.com>.

"Litweb: Baroness Orczy." 2007-05-04.
<http://www.litweb.net/biography/424/Baroness_Orczy.html>.

Quiz 1

1. **What is the port city in France to which the League of the Pimpernel brings its fugitives?**
   A. Venice
   B. Avignon
   C. Paris
   D. Calais

2. **Where is the Fisherman's Edge located?**
   A. London
   B. Cardiff
   C. Dover
   D. Edinborough

3. **Who is captured in Chauvelin's first raid?**
   A. Armand St. Just
   B. Percy Blakeney
   C. Sir Andrew
   D. Lord Antony

4. **Who is Marguerite St. Just in England?**
   A. Lady Blakeney
   B. Mademoiselle Beauregard
   C. Suzanne de Tournay
   D. Comtesse de Tournay

5. **What is the name of the inn in Chalais where Percy and Chauvelin meet?**
   A. West Barricade
   B. Chat Gris
   C. Dover Inn
   D. Fisherman's Edge

6. **Who did Marguerite St. Just condemn to the tribunal council?**
   A. Armand de St. Just
   B. Marquis de St. Cyr
   C. Sir Andrew
   D. Chauvelin

7. **The ball after the opera is held by...**
    A. Lord Antony Dewhurst
    B. Lord Grenville
    C. The Scarlet Pimpernel
    D. Chauvelin

8. **The Scarlet Pimpernel is named after a...**
    A. flower
    B. war
    C. boat
    D. river

9. **When Baroness Orczy did not successfully publish The Scarlet Pimpernel as a book, she published it instead as a...**
    A. radio show
    B. film
    C. play
    D. opera

10. **What is the name of Percy's ship?**
    A. Blakeney Manor
    B. Freedom Runner
    C. Day Dream
    D. Pimpernel

11. **What does Chauvelin find that makes him sure he can entrap Marguerite St. Just?**
    A. a letter from Armand St. Just
    B. a presidential decree ordering the arrest of Marguerite
    C. Percy's Scarlet Pimpernel ring
    D. a letter from Percy

12. **Which is one word not used to describe Percy at some point during the novel?**
    A. boorish
    B. dull
    C. loquacious
    D. fashionable

13. Who does Percy allegedly go to for help to escape from Chalais?

A. Reuben

B. Brogard

C. Degas

D. Reuben's old Jewish friend

14. Who is not rescued from France in the novel's opening?

A. Countess de Tournay

B. The Tournay young daughter

C. The Tournay young son

D. Comte de Tournay

15. What does citoyen mean in English?

A. clergy

B. flower

C. citizen

D. warrior

16. The Comtesse de Tournay forbids her daughter from speaking to...

A. Lady Blakeney

B. Lord Antony Dewhurst

C. Percy Blakeney

D. Armand de St. Just

17. What does Lady Blakeney put on her body before she returns to England?

A. jacket

B. hair clip

C. hat

D. shoes

18. Lady Blakeney is surprised that Percy's study is...

A. messy and dirty

B. a secret chamber

C. neat and orderly

D. empty and silent

19. **Percy secretly hates Lady Blakeney because she denounced...**
    A. The St. Cyr family
    B. Chauvelin
    C. Lord Antony
    D. Sir Andrew Ffoulkes

20. **When Chauvelin goes to the supper room at 1 o'clock looking for The Scarlet Pimpernel, he instead finds...**
    A. Lady Blakeney
    B. Sir Andrew
    C. Degas
    D. Percy

21. **People are surprised that Percy Blakeney married Lady Blakeney because...**
    A. they think she's too poor
    B. they think she's too rich for him
    C. they think she's too good for him
    D. they think he's too smart for her

22. **What do the masses use to execute nobility?**
    A. hanging
    B. drowning
    C. lethal injection
    D. guillotine

23. **What is the nickname for the instrument of death penalty in revolutionary France?**
    A. Jean Pierre de Gallows
    B. Madame de la Guillotine
    C. Axel de la Avignon
    D. St. Therese de Raquin

24. **What is the name of the Seargent who stands guard over the West Barricades?**
    A. Brogard
    B. Chauvelin
    C. Degas
    D. Bibot

25. Percy gets through the West Barricade dressed as...

A. a Russian count

B. a young peasant

C. an old hag

D. a fox

Quiz 1 Answer Key

1. **(D)** Calais
2. **(C)** Dover
3. **(D)** Lord Antony
4. **(A)** Lady Blakeney
5. **(B)** Chat Gris
6. **(B)** Marquis de St. Cyr
7. **(B)** Lord Grenville
8. **(A)** flower
9. **(C)** play
10. **(C)** Day Dream
11. **(A)** a letter from Armand St. Just
12. **(C)** loquacious
13. **(A)** Reuben
14. **(D)** Comte de Tournay
15. **(C)** citizen
16. **(A)** Lady Blakeney
17. **(D)** shoes
18. **(C)** neat and orderly
19. **(A)** The St. Cyr family
20. **(D)** Percy
21. **(C)** they think she's too good for him
22. **(D)** guillotine
23. **(B)** Madame de la Guillotine
24. **(D)** Bibot
25. **(C)** an old hag

Quiz 2

1. **Percy pretends the people in his cart have ___ in order to get through the barricade?**
   A. tuberculosis
   B. measles
   C. smallpox
   D. syphilis

2. **Chauvelin promises to do what with Armand St. Just's letter if he catches the Scarlet Pimpernel?**
   A. publish it in the newspaper
   B. make copies of it for the president
   C. burn it in the fireplace
   D. return it to Marguerite

3. **Lady Blakeney and Percy have how many children?**
   A. one
   B. two
   C. zero
   D. three

4. **The climactic showdown between Percy and Chauvelin takes place at...**
   A. Chat Gris
   B. Versailles
   C. The Fisherman's edge
   D. Pere Blanchard's hut

5. **'Zooks!' and 'Zounds!' are phrases commonly spoken by...**
   A. Lady Blakeney
   B. Chauvelin
   C. Degas
   D. Percy

6. **The book takes place in...**
   A. 1660
   B. 1792
   C. 1845
   D. 1890

7. **Marguerite St. Just tells Chauvelin that the Pimpernel is a...**
    A. an arrogant cad
    B. an irrelevant foreigner
    C. brave and noble man
    D. a catch worthy of marrying

8. **The guillotine reigns supreme at...**
    A. DayDream's ship
    B. Chat Gris
    C. Place de la Grive
    D. Dover

9. **What is the dominant form of landscape around Pere Blanchards hut?**
    A. cliffs
    B. valleys
    C. mountains
    D. dunes

10. **Who is the proprietor of the Fisherman's edge?**
    A. Mr. Pitt
    B. Lord Ffoulkes
    C. Jellyband
    D. Lord Antony

11. **Percy tricks Chauvelin at the Chat Gris with...**
    A. poison
    B. a snuff box
    C. a magic rock
    D. a card trick

12. **Marguerite watches the encounter between Chauvelin and Percy from...**
    A. the stairwell
    B. the attic
    C. the window
    D. the basement

13. **Lady Blakeney finds the ring of the Pimpernel in...**
   A. Chat Gris
   B. Chauvelin's office
   C. The Fisherman's Edge
   D. Percy's study

14. **Lord Grenville is...**
   A. The President of France
   B. The Foreign Secretary of State
   C. The proprietor of the Chat Gris
   D. The President of England

15. **What is the name of the youngest de Tournay daughter?**
   A. Jessica
   B. Suzanne
   C. Mary
   D. Marguerite

16. **What gives Percy away when he's dressed as the Jew?**
   A. his breath
   B. his British accent
   C. his screams
   D. his clothes

17. **What signals that the fugitives have escaped at the climax of the novel?**
   A. a gunshot from the Daydream
   B. a flag raised on the Daydream
   C. fireworks from the Daydream
   D. the landing of the Daydream

18. **Who takes a liking to Suzanne Tournay?**
   A. Chauvelin
   B. Lord Antony
   C. Percy
   D. Sir Andrew Ffoulkes

19. **Who does Sir Andrew view as inane and flippant initially?**
    A. Lady Blakeney
    B. Antony Dewhurst
    C. Percy
    D. Comtesse de Tournay

20. **Who permits the old hag to go through the West Barricades of Paris?**
    A. Seargent Bibot
    B. Chauvelin
    C. the captain
    D. Degas

21. **Whose first words to Marguerite are 'Citoyen St. Just'?**
    A. Chauvelin
    B. Degas
    C. Percy
    D. Comtesse de Tournay

22. **Who is not a member of the League of the Scarlet Pimpernel?**
    A. Sir Andrew
    B. Chauvelin
    C. Sir Antony
    D. Percy

23. **Who challenges Percy to a duel?**
    A. the youngest son of Comte de Tournay
    B. Chauvelin
    C. Sir Antony
    D. Degas

24. **What is the name of Percy's favorite horse?**
    A. Sultan
    B. DayDream
    C. Blakeney
    D. Degas

25. **How many men are in the League of the Pimpernel?**
   A. 3
   B. 10
   C. 20
   D. 100

Quiz 2 Answer Key

1. **(C)** smallpox
2. **(D)** return it to Marguerite
3. **(C)** zero
4. **(D)** Pere Blanchard's hut
5. **(D)** Percy
6. **(B)** 1792
7. **(C)** brave and noble man
8. **(C)** Place de la Grive
9. **(A)** cliffs
10. **(C)** Jellyband
11. **(B)** a snuff box
12. **(A)** the stairwell
13. **(D)** Percy's study
14. **(B)** The Foreign Secretary of State
15. **(B)** Suzanne
16. **(B)** his British accent
17. **(A)** a gunshot from the Daydream
18. **(D)** Sir Andrew Ffoulkes
19. **(C)** Percy
20. **(A)** Seargent Bibot
21. **(A)** Chauvelin
22. **(B)** Chauvelin
23. **(A)** the youngest son of Comte de Tournay
24. **(A)** Sultan
25. **(C)** 20

Quiz 3

1. **Who does Lady Blakeney call an English turkey?**
   A. Chauvelin
   B. Sir Antony
   C. Mr. Jellyband
   D. Percy

2. **How does Marguerite know that Chauvelin is close to catching the Pimpernel?**
   A. she hears it from the Comtesse de Tournay
   B. Chauvelin sends her a letter
   C. she reads about in the newspaper
   D. she receives Armand's letter back

3. **Who is Chauvelin's most trusted henchman?**
   A. Brogard
   B. Seargent Bibot
   C. Sir Andrew
   D. Degas

4. **Who does the Comtesse de Tournay say she never wants to see again?**
   A. Sir Andrew
   B. Lord Antony
   C. Marguerite St. Just
   D. Percy

5. **What prevents Marguerite from sailing to Calais immediately after hearing of Percy's departure?**
   A. a storm
   B. illness
   C. an injured horse
   D. Chauvelin's detainment

6. **Armand's loyalty to the Pimpernel is a secret initially to everyone except...**
   A. Lady Blakeney
   B. Chauvelin
   C. Percy
   D. France

7. Why doesn't Chauvelin arrest Percy right away at the Chat Gris?

A. he's waiting for Lady Blakeney to witness

B. he's waiting for the Daydream

C. he wants Percy to be poisoned

D. he's waiting for Degas to arrive with soldiers

8. Chauvelin says to "find the Pimpernel for ___!"

A. England

B. Percy

C. France

D. Armand

9. Who announces his presence with 'God Save the King!'

A. Chauvelin

B. Lord Antony

C. Degas

D. Percy

10. Baroness Orczy's sympathies as an author tend to be with the...

A. royalty

B. peasants

C. nobility

D. foreigners

11. Who is known as the Cleverest Woman in Europe

A. Lady Blakeney

B. Mary Queen of Scots

C. Suzanne de Tournay

D. Comtesse de Tournay

12. Who is a proprietess of the Fisherman's Edge?

A. Miss Severine

B. Miss Sally

C. Miss Symond

D. Miss Susanne

13. **The French Revolution was a reaction to...**
    A. Impressionism
    B. The spread of Democracy
    C. The Englightenment
    D. Romanticism

14. **Chauvelin says that if the Jew fails to produce Percy, he will...**
    A. beat him
    B. guillotine him
    C. drown him
    D. shoot him

15. **Chauvelin has been sent to England by...**
    A. The Royalty of France
    B. The Republican Government of France
    C. The United States Embassy
    D. The Ambassadors of England

16. **Who asks Sir Andrew to dance at the ball?**
    A. Lady Blakeney
    B. Countess de Tournay
    C. Miss Salley
    D. Suzanne de Tournay

17. **Why does Chauvelin bring the Jew to Pere Blanchard's hut?**
    A. He's afraid he'll bring soldiers
    B. He's afraid he's sick
    C. He's afraid he might turn into a spy for the government
    D. He's afraid he'll make a noise

18. **When Marguerite hears Percy sing 'God Save the King' on the cliff, she believes it is a signal of his...**
    A. arrest
    B. revival
    C. victory
    D. death

19. Who were Robespierre and Danton

    A. Two members of the league of the Pimpernel

    B. Royalty in the de Tournay household

    C. Cousins of Percy

    D. Two members of the Committee of Public Safety

20. Why do Lady Blakeney and Percy Blakeney initially converge in Dover?

    A. To have a dinner at Lord Grenville's

    B. To kill Chauvelin

    C. To bid farewell to Armand

    D. To rescue more revolutionaries

21. Percy is known for what kind of build?

    A. broad-shouldered, muscular

    B. short, stout

    C. sickly, frail

    D. slim, waifish

22. How old is Percy?

    A. 22

    B. 28

    C. 32

    D. 40

23. Who is called the little French Bantam?

    A. the Vicomte de Tournay

    B. Chauvelin

    C. Miss Sally

    D. Degas

24. Who ends the duel between Percy and the Vicomte?

    A. Lady Blakeney

    B. Brogard

    C. Chauvelin

    D. Degas

25. **Who gets to the Chat Gris first?**
    A. Chauvelin
    B. Marguerite
    C. Degas
    D. Percy

Quiz 3 Answer Key

1. **(D)** Percy
2. **(D)** she receives Armand's letter back
3. **(D)** Degas
4. **(C)** Marguerite St. Just
5. **(A)** a storm
6. **(C)** Percy
7. **(D)** he's waiting for Degas to arrive with soldiers
8. **(C)** France
9. **(D)** Percy
10. **(C)** nobility
11. **(A)** Lady Blakeney
12. **(B)** Miss Sally
13. **(C)** The Englightenment
14. **(A)** beat him
15. **(B)** The Republican Government of France
16. **(D)** Suzanne de Tournay
17. **(D)** He's afraid he'll make a noise
18. **(D)** death
19. **(D)** Two members of the Committee of Public Safety
20. **(C)** To bid farewell to Armand
21. **(A)** broad-shouldered, muscular
22. **(B)** 28
23. **(A)** the Vicomte de Tournay
24. **(A)** Lady Blakeney
25. **(B)** Marguerite

Quiz 4

1. **What is the humble wayside flower?**
   A. The blue tulip
   B. The Scarlet Pimpernel
   C. The scarlet tulip
   D. The Blue Pimpernel

2. **What word best describes Brogard?**
   A. offensive
   B. garrulous
   C. mute
   D. controlled

3. **Who slips the note from the Pimpernel to Sir Andrew at the ball?**
   A. Lady Blakeney
   B. Lord Hastings
   C. Chauvelin
   D. Lord Antony

4. **Who is a friend of Marguerite's from school?**
   A. Comte de Chalais
   B. Sir Andrew
   C. Suzanne de Tournay
   D. Percy

5. **Whose point of view dominates the novel?**
   A. Andrew's
   B. Suzanne's
   C. Percy's Chauvelin's
   D. Marguerite's

6. **Chauvelin maintains what kind of build?**
   A. slight
   B. sickly
   C. broad
   D. stout

7. **Where does the Reign of Terror take hold?**
    A. Russia
    B. United States
    C. England
    D. France

8. **To whom did Marguerite denounce the St. Cyr family?**
    A. the President
    B. the Queen
    C. the English Ambassador
    D. the Tribunal

9. **Marguerite claims she denounced the St. Cyr family because she...**
    A. hated the family
    B. lied
    C. was tricked
    D. wanted to get back at Percy

10. **Who is Jellyband?**
    A. the head of the Reign of Terror
    B. the owner of the Chat Gris
    C. the proprietor of the Fisherman's edge
    D. Percy's cook

11. **Who informs Bibot that the old hag was the Scarlet Pimpernel?**
    A. a captain
    B. Chauvelin
    C. Degas
    D. Percy

12. **What is the name of Marguerite's maid?**
    A. Louise
    B. Suzanne
    C. Jellyband
    D. Sally

13. Before marrying, Marguerite used to be...

A. a teacher
B. an actress
C. a cook
D. a politician

14. Everyone thinks Marguerite married Percy for...

A. his money
B. his power
C. his looks
D. his family

15. Who does Chauvelin want to enlist as a spy for his side?

A. Marguerite
B. Degas
C. Percy
D. Armand

16. Who is the Vicomte de Tournay?

A. Chauvelin
B. Suzanne's brother
C. Degas
D. Percy

17. Who is Mr. Pitt?

A. Percy's father
B. the head of the Reign of Terror
C. the former Prime Minister of England
D. the head of the French Republican Government

18. By the time Percy arrives at Dover having rescued the fugitives, he...

A. gotten drunk
B. has changed into new clothes
C. remarried Lady Blakeney
D. fallen overboard

19. **Which social function ends the novel?**
     A. Lord Grenville's ball
     B. The funeral of Chevalier
     C. The marriage of Percy and Lady Blakeney
     D. The marriage of Andrew and Suzanne

20. **Armand St. Just ultimately ends the story in...**
     A. America
     B. England
     C. Calais
     D. France

21. **Percy and Lady Blakeney escape from Chauvelin through...**
     A. Griz Nes
     B. Chat Gris
     C. Dover
     D. Calais

22. **After beating the Jew, Chauvelin sets off in search of...**
     A. Andrew
     B. Marguerite
     C. the Vicomte
     D. Percy

23. **Who is never seen in England again after the rescue of the fugitives?**
     A. Chauvelin
     B. Suzanne de Tournay
     C. Percy
     D. Armand

24. **Chauvelin promises to meet Lady Blakeney at...**
     A. The marriage of Antony and Suzanne
     B. Lord Grenville's Ball
     C. Percy's funeral
     D. The Prince of Wales' Garden Party

25. Who appears first in the novel?

A. Percy Blakeney

B. Chauvelin

C. Degas

D. Comtesse de Tournay

Quiz 4 Answer Key

1. **(B)** The Scarlet Pimpernel
2. **(A)** offensive
3. **(B)** Lord Hastings
4. **(C)** Suzanne de Tournay
5. **(D)** Marguerite's
6. **(A)** slight
7. **(D)** France
8. **(D)** the Tribunal
9. **(C)** was tricked
10. **(C)** the proprietor of the Fisherman's edge
11. **(A)** a captain
12. **(A)** Louise
13. **(B)** an actress
14. **(A)** his money
15. **(A)** Marguerite
16. **(C)** Degas
17. **(C)** the former Prime Minister of England
18. **(B)** has changed into new clothes
19. **(D)** The marriage of Andrew and Suzanne
20. **(B)** England
21. **(A)** Griz Nes
22. **(D)** Percy
23. **(A)** Chauvelin
24. **(D)** The Prince of Wales' Garden Party
25. **(D)** Comtesse de Tournay

ClassicNotes

GrAdeSaver™

Getting you the grade since 1999™

Other ClassicNotes from GradeSaver™

1984
Absalom, Absalom
Adam Bede
The Adventures of Augie
 March
The Adventures of
 Huckleberry Finn
The Adventures of Tom
 Sawyer
The Aeneid
Agamemnon
The Age of Innocence
The Alchemist (Coelho)
The Alchemist (Jonson)
Alice in Wonderland
All My Sons
All Quiet on the Western
 Front
All the King's Men
All the Pretty Horses
Allen Ginsberg's Poetry
The Ambassadors
American Beauty
And Then There Were
 None
Angela's Ashes
Animal Farm
Anna Karenina
Anthem
Antigone
Antony and Cleopatra
Aristotle's Ethics
Aristotle's Poetics
Aristotle's Politics
As I Lay Dying
As You Like It

Astrophil and Stella
Atlas Shrugged
Atonement
The Awakening
Babbitt
The Bacchae
Bartleby the Scrivener
The Bean Trees
The Bell Jar
Beloved
Benito Cereno
Beowulf
Bhagavad-Gita
Billy Budd
Black Boy
Bleak House
Bless Me, Ultima
Blindness
Blood Wedding
The Bloody Chamber
Bluest Eye
The Bonfire of the
 Vanities
The Book of the Duchess
 and Other Poems
The Book Thief
Brave New World
Breakfast at Tiffany's
Breakfast of Champions
The Brief Wondrous Life
 of Oscar Wao
The Brothers Karamazov
The Burning Plain and
 Other Stories
A Burnt-Out Case
By Night in Chile

Call of the Wild
Candide
The Canterbury Tales
Cat on a Hot Tin Roof
Cat's Cradle
Catch-22
The Catcher in the Rye
The Caucasian Chalk
 Circle
Charlotte Temple
Charlotte's Web
The Cherry Orchard
The Chocolate War
The Chosen
A Christmas Carol
Christopher Marlowe's
 Poems
Chronicle of a Death
 Foretold
Civil Disobedience
Civilization and Its
 Discontents
A Clockwork Orange
Coleridge's Poems
The Color of Water
The Color Purple
Comedy of Errors
Communist Manifesto
A Confederacy of
 Dunces
Confessions
Connecticut Yankee in
 King Arthur's Court
The Consolation of
 Philosophy
Coriolanus

For our full list of over 250 Study Guides, Quizzes,
Sample College Application Essays, Literature Essays and E-texts, visit:

www.gradesaver.com

ClassicNotes

GrAdeSaver™

Getting you the grade since 1999™

Other ClassicNotes from GradeSaver™

I, Claudius
An Ideal Husband
Iliad
The Importance of Being
Earnest
In Cold Blood
In Our Time
In the Time of the
Butterflies
Inherit the Wind
An Inspector Calls
Into the Wild
Invisible Man
The Island of Dr. Moreau
Jane Eyre
Jazz
The Jew of Malta
Joseph Andrews
The Joy Luck Club
Julius Caesar
The Jungle
Jungle of Cities
Kama Sutra
Kate Chopin's Short
Stories
Kidnapped
King Lear
King Solomon's Mines
The Kite Runner
Last of the Mohicans
Leaves of Grass
The Legend of Sleepy
Hollow
A Lesson Before Dying
Leviathan
Libation Bearers

Life is Beautiful
Life of Pi
Light In August
Like Water for Chocolate
The Lion, the Witch and
the Wardrobe
Little Women
Lolita
Long Day's Journey Into
Night
Look Back in Anger
Lord Jim
Lord of the Flies
The Lord of the Rings:
The Fellowship of the
Ring
The Lord of the Rings:
The Return of the
King
The Lord of the Rings:
The Two Towers
A Lost Lady
The Lottery and Other
Stories
Love in the Time of
Cholera
The Love Song of J.
Alfred Prufrock
The Lovely Bones
Lucy
Macbeth
Madame Bovary
Maggie: A Girl of the
Streets and Other
Stories
Manhattan Transfer

Mankind: Medieval
Morality Plays
Mansfield Park
The Marrow of Tradition
The Master and
Margarita
MAUS
The Mayor of
Casterbridge
Measure for Measure
Medea
Merchant of Venice
Metamorphoses
The Metamorphosis
Middlemarch
A Midsummer Night's
Dream
Moby Dick
A Modest Proposal and
Other Satires
Moll Flanders
Mother Courage and Her
Children
Mrs. Dalloway
Much Ado About
Nothing
My Antonia
Mythology
The Namesake
Native Son
Nickel and Dimed: On
(Not) Getting By in
America
Night
Nine Stories
No Exit

For our full list of over 250 Study Guides, Quizzes,
Sample College Application Essays, Literature Essays and E-texts, visit:

www.gradesaver.com

Made in the USA
Middletown. DE
06 August 2016